Who Lives in…
THE FOREST?

Who Lives in... THE FOREST?

Ron Hirschi

Photographs by
Galen Burrell

A *WHERE ANIMALS LIVE* BOOK

Dodd, Mead & Company   New York

Text copyright © 1987 by Ron Hirschi
Photographs copyright © 1987 by Galen Burrell
All rights reserved
No part of this book may be reproduced in any form
without permission in writing from the publisher
Distributed in Canada by
McClelland and Stewart Limited, Toronto
Printed in Hong Kong by South China Printing Company
Designed by Charlotte Staub

1   2   3   4   5   6   7   8   9   10

Library of Congress Cataloging-in-Publication Data

Hirschi, Ron.
  Who lives in—the forest?

  (A Where animals live book)
  Summary: Introduces the inhabitants of the forest, such as
rabbits, chipmunks, owls, squirrels, bear, and trout.
  1. Forest fauna—Juvenile literature.   2. Forest fauna—
United States—Juvenile literature.   [1. Forest animals]
I. Burrell, Galen, ill.   II. Title.   III. Series.
QL112.H57   1987   599.0909'52   87-8879
ISBN 0-396-09121-0
ISBN 0-396-09122-9 (pbk.)

For Ethie

Watch
for the
golden birds,
listen for those
that call their
name,

and follow
an old rabbit
as he disappears
beneath the tall,
tall trees.

Chickadee-dee-dee!
Chickadee-dee-dee!
The chickadee sings
a morning song.

Its friendly call leads you
down the rabbit's sunlit path
to where the chipmunk lives.

The chipmunk looks up,
leaps to the ground,
then munches flowers
for breakfast.

Walk quietly past.
Can you hear the chipmunk
crunching?

Look up!
It is the golden
bird, a tanager,
sparkling in
the new day
sun.

Peek through the branches. Can you

see the warbler looking back at you,

the sky-blue bunting
hopping among leaves
that dance in the wind,

or the baby owls,
feathers puffed in the breeze,
cradled in the sturdy
branches?

Chia! Chia!
Chia! Chia! Chia! Chia!
A squirrel's chattering alarm
breaks the morning
stillness.

What does the squirrel see?

Is it the mother bear and her cub,
or the two spotted fawns
hiding in silence?

No! It is a hungry coyote that frightened the squirrel.

The squirrel waits
until the coyote
trots away, then
he scurries down
to his favorite log
to eat pine cones.
He turns each one
like corn on the cob,
dropping tiny scales
as he nibbles
the seeds.

The cone scales
fall like rain into
the trout's clean,
clear creek.

This gurgling stream
makes a path all
its own, flowing
through the trees
to where the old
rabbit's path
leaves the
forest.

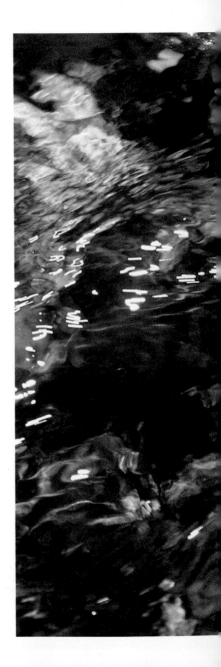

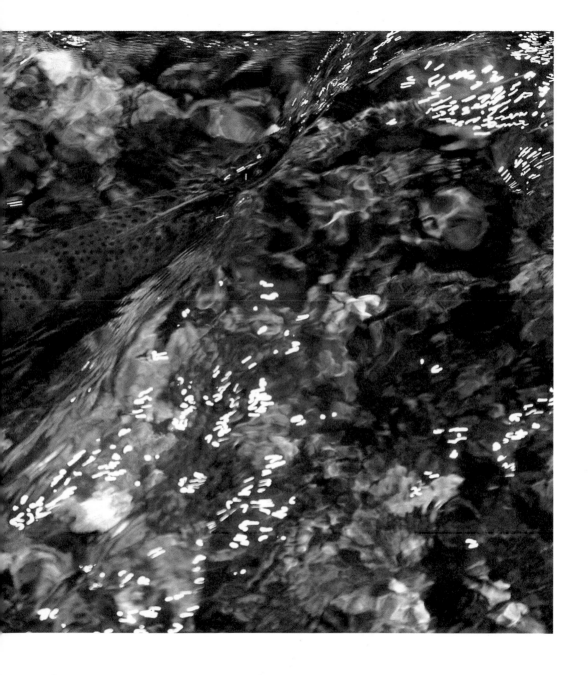

Here, the rabbit
nibbles sweet clover
in the open meadow.

Deep within the forest,
shadows soon fall as mother
owl's soft call brings
an end to this day
in these wild
woods.

AFTERWORD
for Parents and Teachers,
Big Brothers and Sisters

Forests, like individual trees, vary greatly from place to place. So do the animals living within them. Each is as inviting as the Montana aspen, Iowa oak, and Pacific Northwest alder forests that inspired this story.

We can only guess at what young people might think or feel on first hearing a chickadee call its name, seeing the bright flash of a warbler's colorful feathers, or discovering that rabbits really do live in the wild woods. But, we hope this introduction to the forest will help open their eyes, ears, and hearts to these special places.

You might see the animals that appear in *Who Lives in the Forest* in the following places: Look for **rabbits** at the forest's edge. **Chickadees** call their name in forests throughout North America. **Chipmunks** like brushy tangles and tender flowers. The **western tanager** is a beautiful golden bird that lives west of the Rocky Mountains. Many kinds of **warblers** brighten forests all across North America. But, most travel far to the south each winter. **Lazuli buntings** are a great thrill to discover! Look for them in willows along western streams. Listen for **great-horned owls** as evening draws near. **Red squirrels** live in northern coniferous forests and are abundant in Yellowstone National Park where you can also see **black bears.** **Whitetail deer** fawns can be seen within many eastern forests. **Coyotes** search for a meal in many kinds of forest as well as more open land. **Trout** prefer cold, clear streams and benefit from the shade of forest trees.